FIFE BUSES

FROM ALEXANDERS (FIFE) TO STAGECOACH

WALTER BURT

AMBERLEY

Acknowledgements

What an amazing selection of photographs I have had the privilege to choose from. My sincere thanks for their photographic contributions go to Ronnie Cameron, John Openshaw, Barry Sanjana, John Law, Dr George Fairbairn, Innes Cameron, Eddie Taylor, Stephen Dowle, Len Wright, Bryan A. Smith, Martin Addison, Gary Seamarks, Gordon Stirling, Clive A. Brown, Gary Jones, Malcolm Audsley, Paul Green, Andrew Harvey-Adams and especially Robert Dickson. Without people like these, who had the insight to go out and photograph these snippets of time, there would be no book on Fifes buses.

First published 2012

Amberley Publishing
The Hill, Stroud
Gloucestershire, GL5 4EP

www.amberley-books.com

British Library Cataloguing in Publication Data.
A catalogue record for this book is available from the British Library.

ISBN 978 1 4456 0992 8

Typeset in 10pt on 12pt Sabon.
Typesetting and Origination by Amberley Publishing.
Printed in the UK.

Introduction

Let us travel on a journey back through time, to the period just before Walter Alexander's bus company split into the three separate operating companies of Fife, Midland and Northern on 15 May 1961. Here is a brief summery of what happened since then; In September 1963, Scottish Omnibuses Group (Holdings) Ltd, which was renamed from Walter Alexander after the 1961 split, was itself renamed to become Scottish Bus Group Ltd. The group consisted of seven bus companies. They were: Scottish Omnibuses Ltd, Central SMT Co. Ltd, Western SMT Com Ltd, Highland Omnibuses Ltd, W. Alexander & Sons (Midland) Ltd, W. Alexander & Sons (Northern) Ltd and W. Alexander & Sons (Fife) Ltd. These seven companies remained as the Scottish Bus Group until 1985 when the group decided to restructure. It was around 1978 that Fife's buses started to appear with a fleet name style that was to become synonymous with the Scottish Bus Group. Instead of the 'Fife' script name, the Fife Scottish fleet name was appearing with a ¾ Saltire Flag in between the words 'Fife' and 'Scottish'. When the bus group did restructure, four more companies were created along with the fledgling Citylink company. They were the Clydeside, Kelvin, Strathtay, and Lowland Scottish bus companies. It was at this time that the legal lettering of W. Alexander & Sons (Fife) Ltd disappeared from the sides of the buses to be replaced with 'Fife Scottish Omnibuses Ltd'. This is the legal lettering that remains on the sides of vehicles to this day, although the head office has moved from Kirkcaldy's Esplanade to the town's John Smith Business Park. We will start by having a look at some of the vehicles that were operating within Fife in the year leading up to the 1961 split. We will continue to look at some of the various buses, coaches and ancillary vehicles to have served within the Fife company as they were introduced. It is my hope that this book not only appeals to the local bus enthusiast, but perhaps those interested in seeing how the Kingdom of Fife looked between 1960 and the mid-1990s. It is unfortunate that I have been unable to find many images covering buses in the north-east area of Fife. Although mainly in colour, a few good black and white images are also included, mainly because of the subject matter, or to a lesser extent perhaps because there may be something interesting within the photograph itself. Whenever possible, I have included the bus registration and fleet numbers of the vehicles in the photographs, as vehicles may appear more than once in the book with a different registration or fleet number.

Brief History

Since 1909, when the first registered motor bus service ran three times daily each way between Dunfermline and Culross, many small operators began operating bus services throughout Fife. These operators were numerous, and more details can be found in other historical documents and publications. Most of these publications are unfortunately no longer available except through good second-hand book shops, or perhaps the internet. Most of the smaller operators didn't last long though, many being absorbed by the larger operators until they too were absorbed. Gradually, the main operator in the Kingdom became Falkirk-based Walter Alexander & Sons Ltd. Their operations would eventually stretch from Glasgow and Oban in the South and West, to the North East of Scotland. Their operating areas were known as the Southern, Fife and Northern areas. The Southern area subsequently became the Midland operating area after the split.

At this time, all Alexander's buses wore an attractive azure blue livery with one, two, or sometimes three cream relief bands between decks. Their coach livery was 'the opposite' as they were cream liveried, usually with an azure blue roof and relief bands.

At the start of the 1960s, Alexander's buses carried their fleet numbers and garage shed codes on small square plates at the front and rear of each vehicle. The background colour of the plates on the buses which served in Fife was green. The depots which have housed Fife's buses in the duration covered by this book were, or are, at Aberhill (Methil) (AL), Anstruther (A), Cowdenbeath (C), Cupar (CR), Dunfermline (D), Dunfermline Market Street (D2), Glenrothes (G), Kelty (KY), Kirkcaldy (K), Lochgelly (LY), Newburgh (N) and St Andrews (STA). The Fife area head office was on the Esplanade in Kirkcaldy. Dunfermline's Market Street depot was the first to close. This happened in 1961 at the split. Kelty was next when it closed its Oakfield Street doors in 1979. The 1980s saw three closures when, in 1981, Anstruther and Cupar depots closed their doors for the last time, followed in 1982 by Lochgelly depot, which was situated just off Auchterderran Road. There was a trend reversal in 1985 when the new town of Glenrothes opened a depot for business, but it was back to closures again when in 1991, Newburgh depot closed, although it is still used as an outstation.

The bus fleet operated in Fife by Walter Alexanders just before the split consisted mainly of Guy and Leyland vehicles of both double and single-deck types. There was also a sizable fleet of Bristol buses, mainly the LD6G Lodekka, but also twenty single-deck LS buses. Fife was also home to the five Albion Victor buses in the Alexander fleet. The much-loved Gardener engine predominated in Fife's fleet, with the remainder being mainly Leyland. When it was decided to split Walter

Alexander & Sons Ltd into the three companies, the new Fife Company received 516 of the 1,937 vehicles operated by Alexander's at the time.

Fife's buses remained in the Azure blue and cream livery with the only change being to the fleet name with the addition of the word 'Fife'. In 1962, W. Alexander (Fife), as the company had now become, adopted Ayres red and cream for its new livery, with the fleet name simply being abbreviated to the word 'Fife' in a script style of lettering. The 'Bluebird' fleet name for coach services was dropped altogether, although the bluebird emblem was retained. This spelt the end for the Kirkcaldy town service vehicle livery of dark red. Fife's new red livery was basically applied in the same style as the previous blue livery, with the double-deckers having one or two cream relief bands. The single-deckers were now red with a cream waistband and sometimes with cream window surrounds. The coach livery was now cream with a red waistband and roof although the red roof would eventually be phased out.

The first new vehicles to arrive at the new Alexander (Fife) company, still with Stirlingshire registrations, were thirteen LD6G Bristol Lodekka double-deckers, having been ordered before the split up of the company. Eleven Tiger Cub single-deckers were ordered by the new Fife company in the first year, and were still registered in Stirling. Subsequent vehicles would be registered in Kirkcaldy and more about those vehicles will be mentioned throughout the book. Fife made a noticeable purchase in 1968 by being the only Scottish operator to purchase the Bristol RELL6G with Eastern Coach Works bus bodies. They were the only low-floor, single-deck vehicles in Scottish Bus Group service until the 1970s and the arrival of the Leyland National. The Fife Company was also influential in the development of the front-engined Ailsa double-decker, due to its distaste for the rear-engined double-deckers available at the time. Fife was one of the last Scottish bus companies to buy the Leyland Leopard, but from its introduction in 1970, Fife bought large numbers of the type with Alexander's Y-type body, the workhorse of the Scottish Bus Group for many years. (Fife's last new Leopard / Y-type bus, FPE189, is owned by the author).

Fife has been lucky with its bus services throughout the years, in so far as it has never had any serious changes to its operating area. This is due, in no small part, to the geography of the county and its boundaries. The Forth and Tay rivers create natural boundaries at the south and north of the county respectively. We have the North Sea to the east and the Ochil Hills starting in the south-west, stretching north-eastwards along the county border. Indeed, during the 1985 re-structuring of the Scottish Bus Group in preparation for privatisation, of the original group of seven bus companies, Fife was the only company to emerge unscathed from any changes.

Although the Kingdom of Fife is just a small peninsula in the east of central Scotland, it has three main areas within it. The west Fife area, with Dunfermline being the principal town, was an industrial region with its many coalmines and the vast expanse of Rosyth Dockyard, at one time the largest employer on any one site in Scotland, on its doorstep. Most of Fife's busiest services were operating within this area, including the rewarding services to Cowdenbeath, Lochgelly, Lochore and Ballingry. This run has just recently celebrated its 100th anniversary, an occasion for Stagecoach to repaint one of the route's low-floor buses in the old Dunfermline & District tramways colours.

Central Fife, with Kirkcaldy being the principal town, was a mixture of industrial and rural areas and was well served by the many inter-urban services in the area. The Kirkcaldy town services were also busy and frequent.

The north-east Neuk of Fife was predominantly rural with many small towns and villages, with St Andrews and Cupar being the principal towns in the region. It was especially busy during the summer months as this area was a favourite with holiday makers, particularly from the west of Scotland.

As well as comprehensively covering the Kingdom, Fife operated through services to the north, south and west. Glasgow could be reached from St Andrews, Leven, Kirkcaldy and Dunfermline with services run jointly with Midland. The east and north-east of Fife were popular with holidaymakers from Glasgow and the west coast, so these long distance services satisfied the demand. The opening of the Forth Road Bridge in 1964, and the Tay Road Bridge two years later, greatly improved the access for services to Edinburgh and Dundee. Services ran frequently from Dunfermline and Kirkcaldy to Edinburgh and were run jointly with Eastern Scottish Omnibuses.

Since 1991, when Stagecoach took over, there have been many changes to the fleet. The mainstay double-decker was the Leyland (then Volvo) Olympian, with either the Volvo B6 or Dennis Dart as the principal 'Midibus'. Alexander's bodywork usually prevailed on the mainstay buses. The Volvo B10M chassis with Plaxton Premier bodywork has been a good choice of coach for their express network of services. A notable purchase in 1996 was of eight B10 interurban bendi-buses, for use on the Glasgow–Cumbernauld X25 service, which was operated from Dunfermline depot, and two Jonckheere Mistral bendi-buses for Fife to Glasgow services. Other recent purchases have included nine Scania Omnilink tri-axle buses for use on the highly popular Dunfermline to Edinburgh 55 service.

Many bus types have come and gone, some have been successful, some not, and we have seen many changes to the timetables and routes. Certain routes are still there in one way or another, usually shorter versions due to European rules and regulations. But no matter who operates the company, or whatever type of vehicle is running throughout the Kingdom, they will always be Fife's buses.

Dunfermline-based Guy Arab CST5 (RO574) is captured here having just arrived at the town's Carnegie Drive bus stance. We can date this photograph as being after 1961 as the bus at the back has already been repainted into the new Fife colours of Ayres red and cream. Fife's buses were repainted into the new colours from 1962. (*Ronnie Cameron*)

Guy Arab CST5 (FRO574) is pictured again, but sitting in Kirkcaldy at the town's Esplanade bus stance. The destination is a bit of a mystery as route number 302 was a service between Dunfermline and Rosyth Dockyard. CST5 was an acquisition from W. Greig of Inverness in 1947 and lasted until 1966, when it was sold for scrap to Muir's of Kirkcaldy. (*Ronnie Cameron*)

Guy Arab BST171 (RO572) is caught heading down Dunfermline's New Row on a local service, apparently to Woodmill Road. This is another mystery as route number 305 was a run between Townhill and Rumblingwell. This service would not have travelled down this road. Woodmill Road was, however, served by service 375 from the town centre. (*Ronnie Cameron*)

No mysteries here, as Guy Arab BST171 (FRO572) is seen sitting at the rear of Dunfermline depot. This was another vehicle acquired from Griegs in 1947 and was scrapped at Muir's in February 1969. When you compare these first four photographs, you will see that the new Ayres red replaced the blue livery in the same fashion, with the lining being applied in the same style. (*Ronnie Cameron*)

One of only a handful of photographs I have seen of a Walter Alexander bus in the original Azure blue livery. This rear view of WG8805 (P588), a 1939 Leyland Tiger TS8 Special, clearly shows the inclusion of the word 'Fife' on the rear garter, dating this photograph to between 1961 and 1962. It received the 'F' prefix in 1962 to become FP588, but was sold for scrap in December 1963. (*John Openshaw*)

Cowdenbeath Guy Arab 2 AMS310 (RO535), in the service of Walter Alexander, has just arrived at Market Street, Dunfermline, on the busy 314 route from Ballingry. This was before the Alexander Empire split into the three operating areas in 1961, when it seems that wearing a hat was part of everyday normal attire. This vehicle was sold to Muir's in June 1967.

Guy Arab 3 AWG389 (FRO603) sits at the refuelling tank at the St Leonards Street depot in Dunfermline. If this bus was used on a mystery tour, the driver must have had a sense of humour going by the 007 number in the number blind aperture. In the background to the right are the buildings of St Leonards Primary School. It was finally withdrawn in 1970. (*John Openshaw*)

Here we see a 1951 purchase from London Transport in the shape of Guy Arab 2 GYL310 (RO632) sitting at the picturesque St Margaret's Street bus stance. This bus never obtained the 'F' prefix and was sold in March 1963. Not many bus stations will ever have such an imposing backdrop as this. Passengers wait patiently as the driver has time for a cigarette before leaving on the 61 service to Charlestown.

There were five Albion Victor FT3AB buses in Walter Alexander's fleet dating from 1950 which served their entire working lives in Fife. This one, CWG229 (FBA4), is from Cowdenbeath depot and is seen parked up at an unknown location while out on one of Fife's popular tours. This vehicle was withdrawn in 1964, but ended up with the Phoenix Club for the Disabled in Inverkeithing the same year. (*John Openshaw*)

Leyland Titan CCS407 (FRB163) is pictured here parked on the entrance road into its home depot of Lochgelly. This was the former depot of A. R. Forrester's bus company (later Simpson's & Forrester's Ltd), which was absorbed by Walter Alexander in 1938. The depot was demolished in the 1980s. (*John Openshaw*)

AWG710 (FPA35) is a Leyland Tiger PS1 of 1947 vintage with Alexander C35F bodywork. It is pictured here awaiting its next turn of duty on the 311 service to West Wemyss. By the time of this photograph, it did not last much longer in the fleet as it was withdrawn and sold to Muir's in Kirkcaldy in 1968. Muir's scrapyard was the final resting place for many of Fife's buses at this time. A photograph of the scrapyard can be seen later on in the book. (*Robert Dickson*)

At the 1961 split, Fife received ten Leyland Tiger PS1s. DMS831 (FPB18) is seen sitting at its home in Kelty, a depot now demolished. This bus started life as an OPS2/1 but was converted in 1960 by the use of parts from withdrawn PS1s. This bus was withdrawn in 1970, and like many others at the time, ended up at Muir's in Kirkcaldy. (*John Openshaw*)

Leyland PD2/3 DMS502 (FRB142) is caught in the sun on a beautiful day at Dunfermline depot. It was one of sixteen taken in by Fife in 1961 with Alexander bodywork which looked better than Leyland's own body styling. In the distance, at the rear of the bus, can be seen a group of male and female conductors, sitting outside their little wooden hut enjoying the sun. (*Barry Sanjana*)

Fife received all twenty Bristol LS6G buses new in 1955 and all survived until 1973–5. Kirkcaldy's FWG854 (FE19) is pictured here in its home depot. The cream relief band would later be enhanced by painting the side window surrounds cream too. This bus was withdrawn in 1975 and broken up for spares by Alexanders in July of that year. (*John Openshaw*)

Guy Arab LUF JWG508 (FGA17) is seen sitting next to a Leyland Tiger Cub at the back of Kelty depot. This area, near Kelty Cross, is now part of a housing estate and no one could ever imagine there had been a bus depot there. JWG508 was withdrawn and sold to Muir's in 1972. (*John Openshaw*)

Seen with a side roof panel advertising 'Haig in every home', we see Leyland Royal Tiger EMS169 (FPC51) sitting against the sea wall at Kirkcaldy depot. I hope the next driver notices the loosened access hatch near the rear wheel arch! When built, these vehicles had central doors, but were rebuilt with forward entrance doors in 1965. (*John Openshaw*)

Leyland Tiger Cub GWG285 (FPD59) is another vehicle pictured at rest at its home depot in Kirkcaldy. It had been working on the half-hourly local town service number 9 between Brodick Road and Dysart. This was the first of Fife's Tiger Cubs to be withdrawn and scrapped in September 1970 after 'accidental damage'. (*John Openshaw*)

Seen in Dundee bus station during 1976 in the company of Northern's Leyland Titan (NRB216) is Fife's MWG371 (FPD156), a Leyland Tiger Cub of 1959 vintage from St Andrews depot. Notice the 'pay as you enter' sign, displayed when working on a service without a conductor. (*John Law*)

OMS270 (FPD194), a Tiger Cub seen here in the mid-1970s at St Andrews bus station and garage, was new to Walter Alexander as PD194 but shortly thereafter transferred to the Alexander (Fife) subsidiary. This was an Anstruther-based bus and is on a one-man-operated service; hence the 'pay as you enter' hinged board on the front nearside. A sturdy Fifer in a businesslike cap occupies the seat behind the driver. An Alexander-bodied Y-type Leyland Leopard can be glimpsed in the shed behind. (*Dr George Fairbairn*)

Dunfermline-based Tiger Cub KMS478 (FPD109) enters the coastal village of Culross on 29 May 1970 on a run from Falkirk to Dunfermline. The run on the section from Kincardine to Culross involved some of the most demanding driving in the Dunfermline area. Being a conservation area under the auspices of the National Trust for Scotland, little has changed in the village, including the houses seen in the photograph. (*Robert Dickson*)

A Leyland Royal Tiger and a bit of an oddity too. I believe that two of these buses were rebodied to a one-man specification, with one receiving new side windows too. This must be the example that had only the front rebuilt. It is DWG692 (FPC35) and is sitting at its home depot at Cowdenbeath. (*John Openshaw*)

Alexanders never operated any AEC buses in Fife until after the split, when in 1962 Fife received its first batch of twelve in a surprise purchase. 7430SP (FAC10) is seen here parked up in Kirkcaldy depot, having just made a return journey to the town from Dundee. (*John Openshaw*)

AXA222A (FAC22) is seen here at an unknown location, showing the coach door as fitted to the earlier version of these buses. This was one of the first batch of fourteen buses delivered to Fife with the Alexander Y-type body. Note the antimacassars on the head rests of the coach seats, denoting that it must have been on a tour. (*Barry Sanjana*)

Anstruther was home to several Alexander-bodied AECs, another of which is BXA427B (FAC31). It is pictured in the depot yard on 10 August 1978, and would be used later on that day on the local 361 service to St. Andrews, which only took half an hour. It is seen wearing the original coach livery with the red roof, although these were later repainted cream. Note the absence of emergency exit at the rear of this coach as this was the norm when built in 1964. (*Robert Dickson*)

Anstruther's Alexander-bodied Y-type Reliance GXA158D (FAC58) is seen at its home depot. Service 355 ran between Leven and Dundee but a few peak-time runs ended at Crail, heading up the coast. I don't think the corporate-style fleet name suited the coach livery at this time. (*Innes Cameron*)

Fife never had any Bedfords until 1962, when four VAS1s arrived. One had a Duple Midland bus body while the other three had Duple Bella Vista coach bodies. 7435SP (FW3) is one of the latter and belongs to Dunfermline depot. All four Bedfords were withdrawn 10 years later (1972) and were sold on for further use. This vehicle was exported to Antigua in September 1977.

This rather grainy image of LD6G Lodekka GM7002 (FRD106) is included here to illustrate the original long type of front grill. It is seen at rest in Kirkcaldy bus station in between runs on the local service 12 to Birnam Road. Twelve GMXXXX-registered buses came from Central SMT in 1969 and by that time were 14 years old. They were all withdrawn in 1972 and sent to Muir's in Kirkcaldy.

FLF6G Lodekka 7410SP (FRD162) comes off Sinclair Gardens roundabout in Dunfermline from Appin Crescent. Unfortunately, its destination and origin are both unknown, as is the date. What we can observe are the long queue of cars coming off Appin Crescent and the WPC standing at the line of cones. (*Eddie Taylor*)

About a quarter of the way and 7404SP (FRD156) makes light work of the climb up Dunfermline's New Row. At the time, this was the main access to the town centre from the south. It has come from Linburn Road at the south-east of the town, and is heading for Beatty Place, which is off Robertson Road, halfway up the equally steep Townhill Road. You can no longer travel up the New Row by bus at this location (which is the same location as seen in photograph 003). The Dunfermline and West Fife hospital is to the right of the photograph. (*Len Wright*)

One of the buses at Kirkcaldy depot used on the local town services. After 1961, Kirkcaldy still adopted the headboard bearing the 'Town Service' legend. RWG372 (FRD149), an LD6G Lodekka, is seen at rest outside the main shed doors at Kirkcaldy. (*John Openshaw*)

A group of Lodekkas of both LD6G and FLF types, including MMS743 (FRD91) and 7407SP (FRD159), sit waiting their next turn of duty inside the shed at Kelty depot. Note the variation between the application of the cream relief bands, and how the older LD6G model still carries the yellow panel lining. (*John Openshaw*)

3654FG (FRD168), an FS6G Lodekka, is seen at the Esplanade bus stance, the halfway stage of its run from Upper Largo to Dunfermline. The run was about an hour in either direction from here and was usually a busy route. Much of the route today remains unchanged. (*John Openshaw*)

This near side view of HXA412E (FRD212) clearly shows the plainness of the livery as applied at this time, and although plain, it was still an attractive livery. This bus was photographed in April 1981, making it almost 14 years old, and did not last much longer in the fleet as it was sold that year. (*Robert Dickson*)

This bus, YWS871 (FRD156), which was new in 1962, had actually belonged to another SBG subsidiary, Scottish Omnibuses, for the first 12 years of its life. In 1962 'WS' had been an Edinburgh registration mark. Like all SBG Lodekkas, this one has a Gardner LW engine (lucky Scottish drivers!) and, like Lodekkas everywhere, an ECW body. Having just arrived on a duplicate 8 service from Glamis Road, it is pictured at Kirkcaldy bus station on Tuesday 16 May 1978. This bus was eventually transferred to Bristol in 1974. Note the Cave – Brown – Cave intake louvre grills, a feature that Fife preferred not to have on its Lodekka buses. (*Stephen Dowle*)

BXA457B (FRD192) is seen pictured at the terminus at Gallatown, Kirkcaldy during April 1979. It was on local service 1, which was Gallatown to Invertiel by way of Junction Road and the town centre. By the time of this photograph, this FS6B Lodekka was 15 years old. (*Robert Dickson*)

This view of 3670FG (FRD184) sitting at Kirkcaldy bus station must have been planned with the photographer in mind: A nice sunny open position, with no buildings to cast annoying shadows across one's subject. On Tuesday 16 May 1978, with plenty of vehicles such as this Bristol FS6G Lodekka on view, what more could one ask? You could just imagine the aroma of the sun-warmed interior as the folding doors were pushed open. You can almost imagine hearing the ticking of the expanding roof panels. The busman's job might have been quite pleasant if it hadn't been for the need to carry passengers. (*Stephen Dowle*)

This bus is TWG531 (MRD161), a Bristol FLF-type Lodekka of the Alexander Midland subsidiary of the Scottish Bus Group. It is seen swinging out into the traffic from Dunfermline's upper bus station on Saturday 7 May 1977. The bus is heading for Edinburgh on the 55 service. It is probably covering a breakdown in Perth of a Dunfermline bus on the 55, which at that time ran from Perth through Kinross, Kelty and Dunfermline to Edinburgh. (*Stephen Dowle*)

Seen sitting at the back of Dunfermline depot is Bristol FLF Lodekka HXA402E (FRD202). By the end of their days, they were mainly working on school or work contract runs. The Lodekkas did sterling work for the Fife Company, but were all withdrawn by 1981. (*Innes Cameron*)

Nothing seen in this photograph now remains. This is St Leonard's Street in Dunfermline. It was all demolished when the road was widened in the late 1990s. To the left is now the site of an Asda superstore. The bus depot is still there but hidden behind the houses on the right of the photograph. KWG612 (FRD59) is seen on the service to Runblingwell from nearby Izatt Avenue. (*Len Wright*)

With the service now re-numbered from 306 to 7, BXA463B (FRD198) makes light work of the incline up Castlandhill Road in Rosyth on the service to Upper Largo. Little has changed with this scene, with the exception of the bus shelter now being on the opposite side of the road and the occasional chicane to calm traffic. (*Eddie Taylor*)

Seen passing the Adam Smith Centre on its way down to the bus station in Kirkcaldy, we see FLF type Lodekka 7408SP (FRD160) making steady progress towards its ultimate destination of Dunfermline.

'There once was an ugly duckling'. Unfortunately, this type of bus never grew up to become a swan. Introduced in 1963, the Albion Lowlander with Alexander bodywork just didn't look right and was not deemed to be a successful design. The upstairs front seats were raised to accommodate the driver's cab area, which looked like it was between decks. Notice the lack of cream relief bands on Cowdenbeath's 7415SP (FRE2). (*John Openshaw*)

The driver of former Western SMT Lowlander UCS616 (FRE26) has just changed the blind to read 'Edinburgh' in preparation for his next run to the capital. In those days, the low bridge at Jamestown was no worry as the buses turned in a turning area before the low bridge when heading south. This bus, acquired in 1966, was bodied by Northern Counties, which looked better than Alexanders' own bodywork. It survived with Fife until 1977, when it was disposed of to Muir's. (*John Openshaw*)

Former Central SMT vehicle FGM25 (FRE16) is another Northern Counties-bodied Albion Lowlander and is seen at Kirkcaldy depot with the corporate fleet name applied. The fleet number and shed plates are missing, which probably means the vehicle is being prepared for disposal. If so, the fleet name will be removed next.

This photograph sees Alexander Y-type Albion Viking HXA29E (FNV29) having just arrived at St Andrews bus station on a local circular service around the town. This is a compact little combined depot and bus station, but suits the needs of the locality. (*Innes Cameron*)

The east end of Kirkcaldy High Street is the setting for Albion Viking MXA639G (FNV39), seen on service 81A, which was a local run to Dysart from Kirkcaldy railway station. The prices on display in the petrol station to the left were for a gallon of fuel – how times have changed. (*John Law*)

DXA412C (FNV12) waits at St Andrews depot before its next run, which is a part route run to Leuchars railway station. The 355 service had many 'part route' runs incorporated within the timetable as it was almost 2 hours and 20 minutes for the run between Leven and Dundee. This run must have been one-man-operated as it is displaying a 'pay as you enter' notice on the lower nearside windscreen. (*Dr George Fairbairn*)

Travelling west along Appin Crescent in Dunfermline on 3 July 1977 is PXA648J (FRF48) of Cowdenbeath depot. It is an Eastern Coach Works-bodied Daimler Fleetline from 1971. Appin Crescent is one of Dunfermline's busy main roads, and is not so quiet nowadays. The 314 service was the predecessor to the present service 19, serving the same route between Ballingry and Dunfermline. (*Bryan A. Smith*)

Cowdenbeath depot's SXA70K (FRF70) is seen in Carnegie Drive bus station loading up for the return trip to Ballingry. These Northern Counties-bodied vehicles were new to Fife in 1971 when five were delivered. They were all transferred to the Alexander (Midland) company in 1975.

Here we see Daimler Fleetline LXA402G (FRF2) sitting outside the shed doors at Kirkcaldy depot. It has been, or is about to go, on the local 12A town service between Lindores Drive and the town centre.

Sitting in the shed at St Andrews is PXA635J (FRF35), waiting its next turn of duty for the day. Typical of the ECW Bodywork is the white / cream window rubbers, which suited these vehicles. This view shows how compact the depot is. (*John Law*)

Daimler Fleetline PXA635J (FRF35) catches the sun as it passes the ruins of St Andrews Cathedral in 1974. Apart from being the home of golf, St Andrews is a beautiful town with a famous university. It also has its own little depot, which that year housed a good selection of AEC Reliances and Tiger Cubs. (*Dr George Fairbairn*)

Here is an interesting photo of LXA413G (FRF13) sitting around the back at Dunfermline depot. It has been repainted with a large cream band around the body in the area between the upper and lower saloons. There are other photographs later on in the book of Ailsa buses adorned in a similar fashion. (*Robert Dickson*)

Alva is the location for this pair of Fleetlines (FRA14 and 12), having just arrived on a Sunday school outing on 24 May 1980. Alva was always a popular location for outings, not just from Fife, but other areas too. A good variety of buses could be seen during the summer weekends. (*Robert Dickson*)

LXA408G (FRF8) was one of the original twenty buses bought in 1968. It is seen in a rather clean condition, having just arrived on the 89 service from Overton Mains. This service had a 20-minute frequency and ran via the Victoria Hospital. Alexander's Coachbuilders made good use of the Y-type rear window moulding for the upper saloon front windows. (*Martin Addison*)

The SMS – P batch of Fleetlines were far travelled. This bus was new to Alexander (Midland) before moving on to various other owners including Kelvin, Western, Northern and Highland. SMS129P (729) is seen in the beautiful setting of St Andrews, wearing the large logo livery as applied to vehicles around 1987. (*Gordon Stirling*)

A local service within Dunfermline in the charge of LXA415G (FRF15) heading down towards the High Street. On the right is the Andrew Erskine church and on the left of the bus, about 10 yards further up the road, is the entrance to the present-day bus station (Dunfermline's fourth bus station). (*Robert Dickson*)

RXA57J (FRF57) is seen sitting between two Eastern Coach Works-bodied vehicles in the shape of Lodekka FRD201 to the right and ECW-bodied Fleetline FRF43 to the left. ECW vehicles usually had white/cream window rubbers, making them quite distinguishable from other vehicles. (*Robert Dickson*)

Daimler Fleetline VRS147L (FRF78) has just entered Dundee bus station with window stickers displaying 'Wormit' and 'Newport'. This is a mystery to me as that would place it on a run operated by Northern Scottish between Dundee and Gauldry. This is one of three vehicles with Alexander bodywork acquired from Grampian Buses in 1983 with dual doors. It would be converted to single-door soon after acquisition.

Although the RE was fairly plentiful in Scotland, the only ECW-bodied examples were the batch of a dozen or so operated by Alexander Fife, of which JXA924F (FE24), seen here, is an example. The bus was photographed after having unloaded its passengers on a service from Kelty, at Carnegie Drive bus station in Dunfermline, on 7 May 1977. (*Stephen Dowle*)

Aberhill depot's Bristol RE, JXA929F (FE29), is seen sitting awaiting the time for its departure at the bus station on the Esplanade in Kirkcaldy. It must be a very quiet day as the bus is devoid of any passengers for the run back to Kennoway. (*John Openshaw*)

With the adoption of the corporate image logo, JXA923F (FE23) shows how the cream relief band has been applied beneath the natural waistband aluminium strips. The bus has just arrived on a service 38 from Glenrothes. (*John Law*)

XXA855M (FPE55) is captured here having just arrived on a run from Falkirk on 9 April 1981. It is stopped just outside Dunfermline Carnegie Drive bus station to pick up another driver, and is about to make its way down the road to the depot at St Leonard's Street. (*Robert Dickson*)

Fife was a late converter to the Leopard, with the first intake during July 1970. One of Dunfermline's older Y-type coaches is OXA456H (FPE6), which is seen at rest in the depot on 9 April 1981 in the company of FRF13, which was seen in an earlier photograph. (*Robert Dickson*)

FPE6 again, this time on a dull autumn day during November 1981. The pale blue building in the background was the stance café, always a popular meeting area in the town, and as I recall from when I was a little boy, they used to serve a nice glass of orange juice. (*Robert Dickson*)

A quartet of Y-type coaches sit in the rain on a rather wet day in Blackpool. They must be almost ready to leave and head back north as there are passengers seated on all coaches, perhaps waiting for the stragglers to arrive back from a disappointing shopping trip on such a rain-lashed day.

A lovely picture of WXA944M (FPE44) as it winds its way down towards North Queensferry. It has just passed beneath the northern approach viaduct of the Forth Road Bridge, as seen in the top left corner. Buses in North Queensferry turned at the turning area in Battery Road, a hard manoeuvre if a car was parked there illegally (which often happened, and still does). (*Clive A. Brown*)

OXA547H (FPE7) is seen here about to pass beneath the north approach viaduct of the Forth Road Bridge, climbing the hill out of North Queensferry. The spectacular ironworks of the Forth Rail Bridge loom behind this Alexander-bodied Leyland Leopard. This is the same location as the previous photograph but looking in the opposite direction. (*Dr George Fairbairn*)

Leyland Leopard OXA454H (FPE4) sits at the bus stop near Saunders the newsagent's shop, at the east end of Woodmill Crescent in Dunfermline. This was my local bus stop when I was a young lad in the 60s and 70s. I remember passing this stop daily on my seemingly endless trips to Saunders shop, then in my teens on the way to Woodmill High School. (*Innes Cameron*)

Despite the route number and destination displayed on OXA460H (FPE10), this Dunfermline Leopard will probably be on its way to Kirkcaldy workshops on the Esplanade. The engineering staff used to go along this road (Aberdour Road in Dunfermline) on the way to Kirkcaldy via Bernard's Smithy. (*Robert Dickson*)

Fife Scottish Leopard PSX180Y (180) is seen storming up the New Row in Dunfermline on 13 August 1997, on service D4 to Townhill. This bus got transferred to Dunfermline late in its life with Stagecoach and somewhere along the line it gained a one-piece windscreen. The Forth Bridge can just about be glimpsed on the horizon. (*Gary Jones*)

Alexander Y-type Leyland Leopard YSF89S (89) is seen on the local clockwise town service 88 in Kirkcaldy. It is carrying the livery applied when Stagecoach bought the Fife company in 1991. This livery was known as 'Candy stripe' by staff at the time.

Alexander T-type Leopard RSC190Y (290) is seen leaving the bus station at Leven Shorehead. When Fife adopted a new renumbering system in 1988, numbers in the 2xx range were designated for dual seated vehicles. (*Robert Dickson*)

Another Duple-bodied Leyland Leopard is GSG122T (222), seen leaving Market Street bus station on the local service down to the new town of Dalgety Bay. Another dual-seated vehicle with the revised fleet name logo. (*Robert Dickson*)

Duple-bodied Leopard NSU132 (232) is seen with a slight variation to the final fleet name style as the vinyl applied is all red in colour. It is captured here leaving Dunfermline bus station on a Citylink service. (*Robert Dickson*)

Typical of Fife's Y-type Leopards after 1985 is CSF165W (265), which carries the 'Large Logo' style of livery and fleet name. This style was applied to most vehicles as the Fife company readied itself for deregulation. This is another dual-seated vehicle on the busy service 79 to Dalgety Bay. (*Robert Dickson*)

Another Leopard on another run to Dalgety Bay. PSX182Y (182), one of the final batch of new Y-types delivered to Fife without overhead luggage racks, is seen with the 'Bayliner' legend above the side windows. This was to commemorate the 25th anniversary of the new town of Dalgety Bay. (*Robert Dickson*)

Seen drawing away from the stance at Dunfermline on 6 November 1991 is Y-type Leopard GSO92V. It was on hire from Bluebird Buses to Fife at Cowdenbeath depot, covering for a shortage of vehicles, and was operated on the busy 19 service between Ballingry and Dunfermline. (*Robert Dickson*)

At the time this photograph was taken, (about 1989), there were only three runs each way between St Andrews and Edinburgh. CFS110S (210) is seen getting ready to pull into the stance in St Andrews on one of those runs carrying 'Cityliner' branding on the front panel. (*Gary Seamarks*)

WFS138W (138) has just come down the new road of St Margaret's Drive in Dunfermline which cuts through the town's public park. It is on its way to the depot having just come from either Glasgow or Kirkcaldy and terminated at the bus station. Nowadays, you would have to display 'Not in Service' when running light so as not to confuse the public. (*Gary Seamarks*)

Leopard YSF88S (FPE88) is captured parked in the layover area at Glasgow Buchanan Street bus station in 1981. It has just made the arduous 2 hour 35 minute trip on the service 14 from Dunfermline, so the driver is having a well-deserved break before heading back home to Fife. This bus is now preserved. (*John Law*)

Having just reversed out of its stance, Leopard WFS135W (FPE135) is about to embark on its journey to North Queensferry. This route remained largely unchanged over the years, heading through Rosyth via Park Road and Inverkeithing High Street.

Y-type Leopard YSF93S (93) is seen on its way to the bus station in St Andrews, having just completed a short working on the 95 service from Dundee. Perhaps because of the location and the beautiful day, the bus seems to be patronised by a few elderly passengers. (*Gordon Stirling*)

T-type Leopard NFS175Y (FPE175) is caught travelling down Carnegie Drive en route to Kelty Black Road. The bus has just had a 5-minute rest in the bus station having previously arrived on the popular and busy run from Edinburgh.

PSX187Y (FPE187) is seen midway between Cowdenbeath (Kelty Junction) and Kelty on a service 18 run to Beechbank Crescent within Kelty. This is a good photo of the SBG's workhorse in action. (*Clive A. Brown*)

The sun manages to find a way through the clouds and hits NFS172Y (FPE172) broadside on an overcast day in January 1983. FPE172 is a Leopard with Alexander T-type body which was much suited for inter-urban work. It is seen dropping off a few shoppers in Clackmannan's Alloa Road, having come from either Stirling or Glasgow. (*Robert Dickson*)

PSX189Y (189) is pictured here near Kirkcaldy bus station on the 36 service having made the arduous journey from Perth via Newburgh. She was one of a batch of ten new buses in 1982 and was delivered as PE189. This batch of buses was delivered without overhead luggage racks, making them unique vehicles. She was numerically Fife's last new Y-type Leyland Leopard and is currently preserved by the author. (*Clive A. Brown*)

A nice collection of Leyland Leopards sit basking in the sun in the layover area at Dunfermline's Market Street bus station in July 1987. This was the only area in the bus station to get the sun as the main passenger area was north-facing, making it a very dark and dull area most of the time.

CSF167W (267) sits at Stirling bus station having just arrived on the long and arduous journey from St Andrews. This vehicle displays the new fleet number when the company dropped the prefix lettering in the mid-1980s. 267 was a vehicle fitted with dual-purpose seating. (*Clive A. Brown*)

As well as tours, Fife was a great provider of buses for private hires. Alva is the location for this hire as we find at least three Duple-bodied Leopards in evidence. Here we see the difference in styling between the Duple Dominant Mk 1 (FPE118) and Mk 2 (FPE120). (*Robert Dickson*)

Aberhill's Duple-bodied Leopard, GSG123T (FPE123), sits at rest in the layover area at Edinburgh's old St Andrews Square bus station in 1983. It has just arrived on service 57 from Leven via the Fife Coast. A journey time of less than 2 hours will see it back at Leven. (*John Law*)

T-type Leyland Leopard RSC190Y (FPE190) is seen here at Edinburgh St Andrews Square bus station, having just unloaded a selection of packages at the rear. It was common at the time in the SBG to have a package delivered via the various parcel agents. This load would be dealt with by the parcel office within the bus station. (*John Law*)

Dunfermline Abbey is once again the backdrop as Duple-bodied Leopard coach GSG125T (FPE125) is seen having just arrived on a service from Charlestown via Limekilns. If you weren't in a hurry, I don't think anyone would have minded being in such a picturesque setting as this while waiting for a bus.

HSX64N (FPE64) is one of Fife's Alexander M-type-bodied Leyland Leopards used on long haul services to London. These were delivered new in 1975 in a variation of Fife's red and cream livery. They were repainted in 1976 into the corporate blue and white colours which were adopted by all the SBG companies. (*John Law*)

Another visit to St Andrews depot finds us in the company of Y-type Leopard WFS151W (FPE151). It is seen on arrival on the 95 service from Dundee, and will eventually terminate in Leven. (*John Law*)

New in 1982 as FPE172, and pictured here in Kincardine, is Alexander T-type Leopard NFS172Y, renumbered as 272 in 1988. This dual-purpose vehicle carries another slight variation to the new fleet name when photographed in July 1990. It was applied in black, which stood out more when compared to the standard red vinyl. (*Robert Dickson*)

T-type Leopard NFS176Y (FPE176) is photographed at Stirling bus station having just arrived on service 23 from St Andrews on 15 November 1983. It is carrying Fife's Cityliner livery, which was the predecessor to what was to become 'Citylink'. Each of the SBG companies carried this livery with a bit of their own livery included; e.g. Fife's Ayres red is incorporated into the three horizontal lines in the silvery grey waistband. Midland's variation would have been blue within the three lines and so on. FPE176 is now preserved at the Scottish Vintage Bus Museum at Lathalmond, near Dunfermline. (*Robert Dickson*)

XXA862M (FPE62) is pictured crossing the Glen Bridge in Dunfermline on a 378 service to High Valleyfield on 9 April 1981. The white building at the top of the small hill was Dunfermline's fire station, while hidden behind the roof of the bus was the bus station. This scene is, at the time of writing, about to change dramatically with the building of a new supermarket where the bus station once stood. (*Robert Dickson*)

Fife never really took to the Ford chassis, only receiving seventeen between 1974 and 1975. Ten were coaches bodied by Duple, of which AXA302N (FT2) is one. It is seen at rest just up from the esplanade in Kirkcaldy. This coach was transferred to Highland Omnibuses in 1979. (*Innes Cameron*)

Seven Ford chassis were bodied with Alexander Y-type bus bodies. HSF558N (FT13) is pictured here outside Kirkcaldy depot having just done a duplicate service on one of the local runs around Kirkcaldy Town Centre. It would be transferred to Highland Omnibuses in 1982. (*Innes Cameron*)

Another of the Alexander Y-type Fords is HSF562N (FT17), seen at rest at its home depot of St Andrews during the spring of 1981. A year later, this bus would also find itself out of favour with Fife and end up with Highland Omnibuses. (*John Law*)

Seen in the St Margaret's Street bus station in Dunfermline, having just arrived from Rosyth Dockyard on 3 July 1977, is Alexander Fife LSX21P (FRA21), a Volvo Ailsa with Alexander body. Although it is now a car park, nothing much else in this area has really changed. The bus was withdrawn when it apparently broke its back due to chassis corrosion in around 1988–89. (*Bryan A. Smith*)

A quartet of Ailsa buses are parked up in the layover area in Kirkcaldy bus station. This photograph illustrates the various cream relief variations at the time. Second from the left we see one of a batch of buses to receive a large cream area between upper and lower saloons. Some buses had cream areas where advertising posters were placed, while others didn't. The Ailsa on the right is a Mk 2, with the higher driving position noticeable when sitting beside the Mk 1 vehicle on its left. (*John Law*)

An Ailsa Mk 1 from Lochgelly depot is seen sitting at the Esplanade bus stance in Kirkcaldy. It is on service 334 which ran half hourly to Lochgelly, at the depot in Auchterderran Road, via Bowhill. This bus, LSX18P (FRA18), was later converted to become a Fife Council Artbus. (*John Law*)

This photograph of LSX22P (FRA22) leaving St Margaret Drive bus stance in Dunfermline, although not showing the stance layout, I think illustrates the limited space available to manoeuvre buses in this area. Great care must have had to be taken as buses had to reverse within the stance area. This is the vehicle that donated its front peaked roof to Doyen-bodied Leyland Tiger MSU463 (563). (See photograph on page 75)

The miners' gala was an annual event held in Holyrood Park. In the early 1980s the Scottish Coalfields had been decimated but the gala was still a big event, with dozens of Midland, Fife and Western buses parked at Lower London Road, Edinburgh. Mk 3 Ailsa A974YSX (FRA74) was eventually acquired by Cardiff City Transport. (*Gordon Stirling*)

A view which epitomises the Volvo Ailsa as OSC48V (FRA48) is seen making steady progress heading up Dunfermline's New Row in November 1984. Believe it or not, this was the main road into the town coming from the south before they built the much-needed St Margaret's Drive, which cut its way through the town's public park. (*Robert Dickson*)

A photograph of OSC50V (850) taken in Kirkcaldy's bus station to illustrate the large logo livery as applied to this type of vehicle. It was neither non-standard nor standard to have a small white version of the logo above the typical triangular SBG destination display at the time.

This Ailsa, UFS876R (FRA43), is seen just about to exit from the bus station in Kirkcaldy. It is wearing a rather striking all-over advert for 'Landmark furniture warehouses', which at the time was based in Jamestown, Inverkeithing. FRA43 was known to staff as 'The Ghost'. (*Robert Dickson*)

A lovely photo of OSC51V (FRA51) taken in Dunfermline about 50 yards down from the top of the New Row which shows the construction of the Kingsgate shopping centre during the late summer of 1984. The building on the right of the photograph is the Masonic Lodge while the advert on the gable end for the Dunfermline Linen Company is a well-known landmark and has recently this year (2012) been refurbished.

Here we find Mk 1 Volvo Ailsa UFS879R (879) approaching the entrance to Kirkcaldy bus station from the west. The bus carries the wide cream band as applied for the 'large logo', but with the revised version of the logo. The stylised map of Scotland with the arrows in the centre of the logo always reminded me of the British Rail logo (called the 'Arrows of Indecision').

B175FFS (FRA75) is pictured here on 2 November 1984 about to enter Dunfermline's Carnegie Drive bus station when it was barely a month old. It is seen in the original livery it carried when new. I believe it carried a similar livery again after it went to Western Scottish Omnibuses 3 years later in 1987. (*Robert Dickson*)

Definitely a day for staying indoors as B175FFS (FRA75) is seen sitting in Dunfermline on a stormy day in June 1986. This was one of two Volvo Citybuses with Alexander's RVC-type coach bodywork delivered to Fife in 1984. As previously mentioned, this vehicle, along with sister FRA76, was transferred to Western Scottish buses in 1987. (*John Law*)

Here we see B176FFS (FRA76) ready to pull out of Glasgow's Buchanan Street bus station on a well-patronised service back to Glenrothes. Those with sharp eyes will have noticed the slight variation to the livery near the rear of the bus and the much reduced application of red below the lower saloon windows. (*Malcolm Audsley*)

Fife's first ten Ailsa buses went to Highland Scottish around 1980. Nine of the original buses returned with a former Midland Ailsa which replaced KSF8N when it was destroyed by fire while with Highland in 1984. LSX10P (810) was one of the buses to return to its home territory in 1991 and is seen on a service to Dundee.

Dunfermline's Citybus C793USG (FRA93) was chosen in 1987 to be repainted into the colour thought at the time to be close to that used by the Dunfermline & District Traction Company Ltd. It was to commemorate the 50th anniversary of the last day of the trams in the area. If memory serves me well, this bus ran a free service all that day (4 July 1987).

This photograph can be summed up with one well known advertising slogan – 'Does exactly as it says on the tin'. The best way to describe OSC60V (860) in my opinion, as the Ailsa really was a workhorse. It did its job, as can be seen in this typical image taken on a service to the Kingdom centre in Glenrothes.

C807USG (907) is caught on the express service from Glenrothes to Glasgow about to enter Dunfermline bus station during May 1991. It was around this time that vehicles used on longer distance services carried a couple of red bands between decks. This was a double-decked coach, as you can just notice the coach seats through the windows. (*John Law*)

Ailsa Mk 1 LSX20P (FRA20) sits in the layover at Kirkcaldy bus station during September 1982, wearing a mid-saloon wrap-around advert for Laidlaw car dealership, a major Ford dealer at the time. (*Robert Dickson*)

B185FFS (985) is seen in large logo livery as applied to the fleet in the mid-1980s. It is waiting to leave from Kinross Sunday market with a healthy load of shoppers on 18 September 1988. The destination is Kirkcaldy, but it will take in a lot of other places en route back to the 'Lang Toun'. (*Robert Dickson*)

Fife adapted the 'Cityliner' branding that was being tried out at the time and applied it to certain vehicles used on the runs to Edinburgh from Leven via the Fife coast. The finished branded livery was 'Fife Coastliner', as carried by C794USG (914) on 5 May 1988, and was not too displeasing to the eye. (*Robert Dickson*)

Racing towards the Kincardine Bridge is C807USG (807) on the X26 service from Glasgow to Glenrothes. This bus was often used on the express services as it was fitted with coach seats. The road layout here has changed since the building of the other bridge near Kincardine known as the 'Clackmannanshire Bridge'. (*Robert Dickson*)

Volvo Citybus C807USC (FRA107) is seen loading passengers at Leven Shorehead bus station on 18 October 1986. It carries the exact same livery as applied to RVC type FRA74, as shown elsewhere in this book, so it was perhaps used a lot more often on the long distance routes at the time. (*Robert Dickson*)

Here's a powerful beast in the shape of Alexander-bodied D10M-50 citybus E909KSG (909). It was used on express services and can be seen here about to leave Kirkcaldy bus station on an express service to Glasgow. It carries the typical livery as used on these coach-seated double-decker buses and was also fitted with a bracket to attach a notice below the windscreen showing 'The Garden Festival'. The service extended beyond Buchanan Street to the garden festival when it was hosted by Glasgow in 1988. (*Robert Dickson*)

A beautiful spring day with a rare blue sky sees Ailsa OSC65V (FRA65) leave with a healthy load on a local service to Chapel West in April 1981. This bus is seen in a variation of the normal livery in that it is sporting a large cream band between decks. There were other vehicles appearing in this livery in around 1980–81. There are photographs of Daimler Fleetlines wearing this livery elsewhere in this book. (*Robert Dickson*)

Fife used to run buses to the popular Sunday Market at Kinross from Dunfermline and Kirkcaldy. There must have been services from outwith Fife to the market, going by the other double decker in the photograph. Dunfermline's UFS875R (FRA42) is seen sitting outside the main entrance on 6 April 1986 having just dropped off a busload from the ancient capital. (*Robert Dickson*)

RSG823V (FPN23) is one of the 11.6-metre National Mk 2s, without a roof-mounted heater pod. It is seen here within the confines of Lochgelly depot. Two of this batch of buses were fitted with different engines for comparison trials. FPN17 was fitted with a Gardner 6HLXB engine, while FPN19 had a Volvo THD100 engine installed. (*John Law*)

The first (numerically) of the first batch of thirteen Leyland Nationals to serve in Fife, HSC101T (FPN1) is seen about to depart from Kirkcaldy bus station on a local run to Chapel West at Ellon Road. FPN1 was an 11.3-metre-long Mk 1 with roof pod, seated fifty-two, and was new in 1978. (*John Law*)

RSG821V (321) was a National Mk 2, new in 1979 with an 11.6-metre body and no roof pod. There were twelve of these fifty-two-seat buses and they were used primarily on the Ballingry to Dunfermline service 19. It can be seen that this vehicle has been fitted with an alternative air intake system to aid engine cooling. This was a Cowdenbeath-based vehicle and is seen at rest at its home depot yard.

This photograph captures Leyland Nation Mk 2 YSX934W (FPN34) in November 1991, leaving Dunfermline bus station on the 74 service to the District General Hospital, now called the Queen Margaret Hospital. It provided access to the new hospital from the estates on the south of Dunfermline and was painted in this dedicated livery. (*Robert Dickson*)

YSX931W (331) is pictured on one of Dunfermline's local services wearing one of the Scottish Bus Group's advertising slogans of the time. 'Best Bus in the Kingdom' was one slogan adopted by Fife which displayed the fact that Fife was proud to be known as a Kingdom because of its history. (*Gary Seamarks*)

The entrance to Dunfermline bus depot is on the right of this photograph as short Leyland National Mk 2 YSX931W (FPN31) passes by with a local service to Rumblingwell. The '5' on the wall is actually a sign saying 5 mph as a reminder to drivers of the speed limit within the bus depot. (*Robert Dickson*)

YSX929W (FPN29) is captured here as it passes the entrance to Dunfermline bus depot at St Leonards. Compare the lack of houses on the opposite side of the road with the previous picture. The houses were slowly purchased and knocked down to make way for the construction of the present dual carriageway in this area. (*Robert Dickson*)

Another picture of FPN29, taken on 2 November 1984, in another interesting place. It is seen turning out of Dunfermline's High Street and heading down the New Row. In the background can be seen the framework under construction for the new Kingsgate Shopping Centre and Marks & Spencer store. (*Robert Dickson*)

St Andrews always turned out immaculate-looking buses, YSX933W (333) being no exception. It is seen sometime around 1990 during a beautiful late spring day on local service 10 to Bogward via Canongate, and is trying to leave the kerbside having just uplifted a passenger. A tour bus had been sitting in the bus stop. (*Gordon Stirling*)

During the period 1986 to 1988, Rennies of Dunfermline operated services in the Dunfermline area on similar or identical routes as Fife Scottish. One such service can be seen opposite Dunfermline depot on the route R5 to Abbeyview. The Fife Scottish service 74 is at the back. People must have been confused as you can see that the Rennies' Leyland National Mk 1 is painted in the exact same way, and in almost the same colour, as the Fife Mk 2 National. (*Paul Green*)

A669XGG (564) is a Leyland Royal Tiger with Roe Doyen bodywork, and is seen in its original condition when working a Citylink service from the Kingdom of Fife to Edinburgh during the spring of 1991. (*John Law*)

Parked up at an unknown location while touring is sister vehicle MSU463 (563). The front of this coach was rebuilt at the workshops at Kirkcaldy after a front-end collision. It has the front peaked dome from Volvo Ailsa LSX22P (FRA22). After the rebuild it was notorious for leaking at the front when it rained. This is another version of coach livery tried out by Fife Scottish. (*Andrew Harvey-Adams*)

One of Fife's first three modern Leyland Tigers, SFS582Y (FLT2) is seen at Kirkcaldy depot in 1983 when new. They wore this livery for use on the dedicated overnight service from Fife to London. They were rarely seen during the day but were used occasionally if there were vehicle shortages. (*John Law*)

Three years later and FLT2 is seen again inside the shed at Kirkcaldy depot. By this time, it has been repainted into the new Scottish Citylink colour scheme of yellow with dark and light blues which I believe suited the Duple Goldliner 3 bodies. (*John Law*)

At one time, this coach was SFS583Y (FLT3), a Leyland Tiger with Duple Goldliner 3 bodywork. It had had a bit of an overhaul by the time it was photographed here in Edinburgh bus station. Gone are the sloping windows, which have been replaced with a more Duple Dominant type of window arrangement. It is unknown if the vehicle had received some form of body damage to warrant a change in style like this.

Another coach in an alternative guise. GSU343 (543) is seen here parked up at Perth bus station in around 1990. This Duple Laser-bodied coach arrived from Highland Scottish in 1987 as A506PST and became FLT28 for a short time before being renumbered to 543. (*John Law*)

Dunfermline's D517DSX (FLT17) is one of the P-types with sixty-one seats that arrived early in 1987. It was used on longer services such as the 55 from Edinburgh pictured here, and will take about half an hour to arrive in Kelty. Not all buses terminated in Kelty, though, as every alternate bus during the day ran on to Perth. Not an unpleasant route, but it could be quite demanding at times.

Alexander P-type Tiger D713CSC (413) is seen entering Kirkcaldy bus station on a service, 321, which mirrored a rival service operated by independent Kirkcaldy-based operator Orion. There was an anti-clockwise service from Kirkcaldy calling at Cardenden, Cowdenbeath, Dunfermline, Inverkeithing, Dalgety Bay and Burntisland. The clockwise service was numbered 123. Orion started the service in 1992, just after Stagecoach took over the Fife company, but could not cope with this competitive service and ceased operating. Both operators' services used conductors.

MNS10Y (470) was one of five Leyland Tigers with Alexanders TE-type bodywork to find its way into the Fife fleet from Kelvin Central buses in 1989. They were fitted with forty-nine dual purpose seats apart, from 470 which was fitted with forty-seven seats. I remember this bus in its later days, when it was the shift bus on the service 80 between Dunfermline and North Queensferry. It had a distinctive wobble to it when accelerating up to 40 mph.

D521DSX (FLT21) was one of the last four P-types ordered by Fife and was slightly shorter than the previous order, having only fifty-seven seats. When compared to the photograph of FLT17, you will notice the absence of the short window bay after the rear emergency door. The location is Dundee's Seagate bus station, and the driver is very busy loading up the shoppers for their return journeys to the Kingdom. A full load like this was never a problem for these buses. (*Malcolm Audsley*)

B208FFS (FLT8) is seen on the 76A service to Crombie, having just come down Pilmuir Street from Wellwood to the north of Dunfermline. It will arrive at the bus station in about a minute on one of the rare local services to use the bus station on a through run. Other local services ran through James Street, behind the bus station. (*Robert Dickson*)

Sister vehicle B209FFS (FLT9) is a Cowdenbeath-based machine, but it is seen here withdrawing from a stance in Glasgow's Buchanan Street bus station. It was not uncommon to find Cowdenbeath buses being used on a Citylink service such as this one, heading for Edinburgh. (*Gordon Stirling*)

B211FFS (511) is a St Andrews depot machine and is wearing an alternative version of the livery seen in the previous two photographs. It will shortly be heading back to its home at St Andrews on a limited stop X99 Cityliner service from Glasgow Buchanan Street bus station in August 1989. (*Malcolm Audsley*)

A pair of Duple Laser-bodied Leyland Tigers is seen sitting near the fuel tank at Kirkcaldy depot wearing liveries with slight differences between them. GSU343 (543) is on the left with a red roof, no red waist stripes and the revised fleet name style of vinyls. GSU344 (544) on the right has no red roof, but has the red waist stripes. They are both sitting beside Q204XSC (1034), Fife's AEC Matador tow truck, in July 1991. (*Malcolm Audsley*)

Leyland Tiger MNS7Y (467) of Cowdenbeath depot finds itself relegated to local town service work around Kirkcaldy. The Stagecoach 'candy stripe' livery surprisingly suited this type of vehicle, which would normally be found on inter urban services. Perhaps it has just recently been transferred to Kirkcaldy from Cowdenbeath, as it still has the Cowdenbeath depot code, which was included in the Fleetnumber at this time. (*Gordon Stirling*)

A987FLS (FRO7), seen here leaving Kirkcaldy bus station on 8 April 1985, stirs up memories of the old Guy Arab buses with the reintroduction of the FRO prefix to the fleet number. This is a Leyland Olympian with Alexander R-type bodywork to a low bridge specification. Ten were delivered in 1983 and were Fife's first double-deckers with Alexander's new R-type of body. (*Robert Dickson*)

Another of Fife's first batch of Leyland Olympians is seen here heading towards Kirkcaldy bus station in March 1988. A984FLS is seen here having recently been renumbered from FRO4 to 784 and in the large logo livery of the time. All of these Olympians were sold on before Stagecoach took over in 1991. (*Gary Seamarks*)

One of ten dual-doored Leyland Atlanteans brought to Fife in May 1984 from Grampian Regional Transport is NRG160M (FRN2), which entered service in August of that year. It is pictured turning from Pilmuir Street into Carnegie Drive in Dunfermline having just taken a load of kids to Queen Anne High School further back up the road. (*Robert Dickson*)

NRG160M (FRN2) is pictured again, this time sitting behind the depot at Dunfermline having been adorned with new 'Best Bus Around' vinyls. It is a year later (1985), and the bus has now been converted to single-door use. (*John Openshaw*)

Another of the ex-Grampian Leyland Atlanteans is NRG162M (FRN10), again seen at Dunfermline Depot. The sharp eyed, and those 'in the know', will have noticed that the fleet numbers didn't match the number plates, as was so often the case with used vehicles. (*John Openshaw*)

Renault Dodge Minibus E811JSX (11) had just passed the Carnegie Leisure Centre when photographed in Pilmuir Street, Dunfermline during May 1991. The D4 was one of the local town services which criss-crossed through the town. (*John Law*)

Here we see Renault Dodge Minibus E813JSX (13) as it turns down Bonnar Street having just departed from around the corner in James Street, Dunfermline. James Street was the departure point for the local services within Dunfermline, a lot of which were 'circular' routes around the town's estates. (*Robert Dickson*)

E320NSX (20) is seen in Dunfermline's James Street in August 1989, a time when Fife, and the Scottish Bus Group as a whole, had bought the minibus in droves to be ready for the imminent invasion by private bus companies on tendered services. In the Dunfermline area, only Rennies provided any real competition, but were soon seen off. (*Malcolm Audsley*)

It is still August 1989 as we see G23CSG (23) loading passengers at stance E on James Street. It is on service 74A, which was a circular route to Abbeyview, in competition with the Rennies service bus seen behind. Rennies couldn't match the competitiveness of Fife Scottish and ended their services rather abruptly soon afterwards. (*Malcolm Audsley*)

MCW Metrorider F56RFS (56) is caught travelling en route to Chapel Village on local town service K2 in Kirkcaldy. These vehicles were new in 1988 and seated twenty-five people. They worked most of their lives with Fife around the Kirkcaldy area, although I believe one ended up in Dunfermline. (*John Law*)

MCW Metrorider F70RFS (70) is seen pictured here at the Clydeside Scottish depot of Inchinnan in attendance at an open day on 10 September 1988. Clydeside became a part of the Scottish Bus Group in 1985, when it was formed from part of Western's northern operating area. (*Robert Dickson*)

The first buses ordered by the new Stagecoach-owned company were twenty-five Leyland Olympians with Alexanders RL-type bodywork in June 1992. K709ASC (709) is at rest within the confines of Cowdenbeath depot having just completed some local trips on the 20 service. These buses were primarily used on the busy 19 service linking Ballingry and Dunfermline.

The Volvo B10M interurban coach with Plaxton Premier bodywork was the main express coach bought in large numbers by Stagecoach, soon after they had bought the Fife company. M953TSX (553) is one such example and is seen in Glasgow before departing back through Fife to Dundee on the X24 via Dunfermline and Glenrothes. (*Barry Sanjana*)

This photograph brings us more or less up to date with Stagecoach, as a recent purchase was for nine Scania Omnilink tri-axle buses for use on the prestigious Dunfermline/Dalgety Bay to Edinburgh services. SP57CNF (24002) is captured here at Ferrytoll Park and Ride, just south of Inverkeithing, loading up before heading to the capitol on one such service.

This photograph, taken at Dunfermline depot on a wet and miserable day, has been included to illustrate the livery and fleet name variations when Stagecoach took control of the Fife Scottish company in 1991. In the background is Dunfermline High School, itself about to become a thing of the past as the new school, built at the back of Dunfermline depot, is almost ready for occupation at the time of writing.

Moffat & Williamson provided the competition for Fife Scottish in central Fife from the 1980s, running services from Kirkcaldy and Glenrothes bus stations. Alexander Y-type Leopard GMS301S is seen at Kirkcaldy bus station in 1991, and is typical of Moffat & Williamson's fleet of the time, mirroring the same type of buses used by Fife Scottish.

Rennies provided the competition for Fife Scottish in the Dunfermline and west Fife area from the mid-1980s. Parked up at the layover area at Dunfermline bus station is OCU768R, an MCW-built Scania Metropolitan typical of the vehicles used by Rennies on the competing services. It arrived from County Travel of Leicester in July 1987, a time when Rennies' bus fleet was forever changing. (*Clive A. Brown*)

Dunfermline-based drivers will recognise this location immediately as being the rail bridge at Merryhill Cottages near Charlestown, on the route from Crombie to Dunfermline. Many a bus has had a new paint job, or a panel repaired, because of the tightness of the turns at both ends of this bridge. Rennies' Duple-bodied Leopard RYJ887R, an ex-Southdown vehicle, is caught negotiating this bend one Sunday afternoon in 1988 on a tendered Sunday service. (*Gary Seamarks*)

I'll bet that whenever this bus gets to Kirkcaldy, there will be somebody there asking why the bus was late. Four buses find themselves snowbound in Aberdour, unable to go any further as the first thing you come to when leaving Aberdour heading north is Donkey Brae, a very, very steep hill with a bad bend halfway up. (*Gordon Stirling*)

Here we see former Guy Arab AWG384 (FRO598), converted to towing vehicle number L7, in December 1964. It is sitting at the rear of its home depot at Dunfermline late on a beautiful sunny afternoon. It should be noted that in the 1960s, breakdown trucks were painted in company colours. (*Barry Sanjana*)

Seen here at Kirkcaldy depot is CWG50 (T2). It is a Leyland PD2/1 and used to carry the fleet number FRB72. It had been painted a rather bland grey for its new role as a driver training vehicle in November 1970. It was withdrawn the following year and scrapped at Muir's in Kirkcaldy. (*Barry Sanjana*)

Another driver training vehicle, also pictured at Kirkcaldy depot, is Guy Arab 2 AMS211 (T1). This vehicle used to carry fleet number FRO504 and is also painted in the drab grey colour applied to training vehicles. It was converted in November 1967 and was withdrawn to Muir's in 1971. It ended up in preservation near Burton. (*Barry Sanjana*)

Kirkcaldy-based breakdown wagon A18AXA (L5) is sitting near the front of the main shed at Kirkcaldy depot in the company of a grey-coloured driver training vehicle. It is believed to be former Leyland PS1 CWG342 (FPA215), which was converted to a tow wagon in 1964 before being moved on to the civil defence the following year. (*John Openshaw*)

This tow truck used to be GWG984 (FRD8), a Bristol Lodekka LD6G. It was converted to a recovery lorry in July 1972. This bus was new in 1956 with Alexanders and spent its entire working life in Fife. It is pictured at its home depot of Kirkcaldy on 20 July 1980, wearing Fleetnumber L5 and plate A18AXA. (*Robert Dickson*)

Like all bus companies, Fife needed to train new drivers and use was always made of former vehicles in this role. Bristol Lodekka 3646FG is photographed meandering along Kirkcaldy High Street on 17 April 1981. The bus was new to Fife in May 1963 as FRD170, but now carries the Fleetnumber T2 (The letter 'T' denoting the bus in use as a training vehicle). (*Robert Dickson*)

Many Y-type Leopards have been converted to work as breakdown wagons and XXA851M was no exception. Formerly FPE51, it carried the Fleetnumber 1051 and was based at Dunfermline depot. It is seen here parked up near stance 1 at the old Market Street bus station while the engineer attends to a problem on a vehicle nearby. (*Gary Seamarks*)

This view taken on 25 April 1983 shows a line-up of withdrawn vehicles at the rear of Midland's Alloa depot. The vehicles are mostly Y-type Leopards with a couple of Bristol RELLs thrown in for good measure. It is not known if these vehicles were heading for the scrapheap or waiting for new owners. (*Robert Dickson*)

What better way to end a book than to show some buses at the end of their lives. In the foreground of this photograph are Leyland Tiger Cubs FPD224/7/30/3/2. They were all new to Alexander (Fife) in July 1961 and ended their days with the company. They are pictured here in April 1978 in the company of at least five Bristol Lodekkas and another Tiger Cub at the rear of the view. (*Robert Dickson*)

This is how quite a lot of Alexander's Fife fleet came to the end of their lives. This is Muir's scrapyard at Randolphfield, Kirkcaldy on 13 April 1979. Albion Lowlander UCS622 (FRE37) had been languishing in the yard for less than a year and is already looking in a pitiful state. At least it made it into the corporate image era with the Fife Scottish logo. (*Robert Dickson*)